SRA OPEN COURT READING

Comprehension and Language Arts Skills

Level 2

SRA

A Division of The McGraw·Hill Companies

Columbus, Ohio

www.sra4kids.com

SRA/McGraw-Hill

A Division of The **McGraw·Hill** Companies

Send all inquiries to:
SRA/McGraw-Hill
8787 Orion Place
Columbus, OH 43240-4027

Printed in the United States of America

ISBN 0-07-570201-0

6 7 8 9 POH 06 05 04 03

Table of Contents

Unit 5 Courage

Unit 6 Our Country and Its People

Common and Proper Nouns

Nouns name persons, places, or things.

Rule	Example
▶ A **common noun** names a person, place, thing, or idea. Common nouns do not begin with a capital letter.	▶ dancer, country, car, color, happiness
▶ A **proper noun** names a certain person, place, or thing. Proper nouns begin with a capital letter.	▶ Dr. Green, America, English

Underline the proper nouns in each sentence.

1. We saw a white tiger at the Columbus Zoo.

2. Tigers live in Asia.

3. Black leopards are found in the Far East.

4. The Ringling Brothers Circus has lions and tigers.

5. Ziggy, the zookeeper, feeds the big cats.

6. Aunt Sue said that tigers are bigger than lions.

Practice

Read the story below. Underline the common nouns.

My name is Lara. I am a tiger from Russia. The zoo where I was born sent me to my new home in California. At first I was homesick, but now I like San Diego. I can smell the Pacific Ocean when I wake up.

Proofread

Read the paragraph below. Underline with three lines (≡) letters that need to be capitalized.

We went to the zoo in florida on saturday. We saw six elephants and two giraffes. I liked the zebra named zig zag. My brother liked the birds the best. There was a parrot named bill. I love going to the zoo.

Compare and Contrast

Focus Writers sometimes use comparison in a story to make an idea clearer.

> ▶ To **compare** means to tell how things, events, or characters are **alike** in some way.
>
> ▶ To **contrast** means to tell how things, events, or characters are **different.**
>
> ▶ Clue words help show how things are alike and different:

Clue Words

Alike		**Different**
both	as	different
same	too	but
like		

Identify

1. Read page 26 of "Come Back, Jack!" What comparision is made between the little girl

   and the rest of her family? _____

   _____

2. Read page 29 of "Come Back, Jack!" What did the little girl and Jack do that is alike? _____

   _____

Practice

Circle whether the sentence is comparing or contrasting. Write the clue word on the line.

3. Jack went into the castle. Jill went into the castle too.

Compare   Contrast _____

4. The little girl laughed, just like Jack.

Compare   Contrast _____

Apply

Think about "Come Back, Jack!" List one way that Jack and his sister are alike.

5. _____

_____

List one way that Jack and his sister are different.

6. _____

_____

COMPREHENSION

Name _____ Date _____

Subject and Object Pronouns

Subject pronouns take the place of the subject of a sentence. **Object pronouns** take the place of the object of a sentence.

Rule
▶ The subject pronouns are:
Singular: I, you, he, she, it
Plural: we, you, they

▶ The object pronouns are:
Singular: me, you, him, her, it
Plural: us, you, them

Example
▶ **I** know that dogs and wolves are related. **They** are both good hunters.

▶ My dog will like **you.** The puppies made **us** laugh every day.

Write a pronoun to replace the underlined nouns in each sentence.

1. <u>Clara Barton</u> was a teacher in New Jersey. _____

2. <u>You and I</u> know that she founded the Red Cross. _____

3. The Red Cross helped <u>my family</u>. _____

▶ **Subject and Object Pronouns**

GRAMMAR AND USAGE

Practice

Circle the subject pronouns and underline the object pronouns in the paragraph.

My name is James Cook, and I am a sailor. In 1768, I became the captain of a ship. I burned vinegar and gunpowder on my ship, because they purified the air. I made the sailors eat fruit to help them stay healthy. They thanked me for caring about them.

Proofread

Read the paragraph, and replace each underlined noun with the proper subject or object pronoun.

Christopher Columbus sailed to America, and

Christopher Columbus _____ started

colonies there. Many explorers traveled across

the Atlantic Ocean, and the explorers _____

saw new lands. We read about the explorers

_____ in history books.

UNIT 1 · **Sharing Stories** • **Lesson 2** *Come Back, Jack!*

Time and Order Words

You can tell when something happens by using time and order words in your writing.

Rule	**Example**
▶ Words such as *yesterday*, *tonight*, and *next week* show time.	▶ We can see Polaris, the North Star, **tonight.**

You can show how something happens by using order words.

▶ Words such as *first*, *next*, and *finally* show order.	▶ **First**, place your apples in the basket. **Then** weigh them on the scale.

 **Write the time or order word from each sentence on the line.**

1. Yesterday, we learned about our history. _____

2. First, we learned that the first president served in 1789. _____

3. Tomorrow, we will study the states. _____

4. I will read more about history tonight for homework. _____

▶**Time and Order Words**

Practice

Underline the time and order words in each sentence.

5. Tomorrow, my class will talk about our pets.

6. Tonight I will write what I want to say.

7. First, I will tell my pet's name.

8. Then, I will say that he is a dog.

9. Finally, I will show a picture of my pet.

10. After school, I will take my dog for a walk.

WRITER'S CRAFT

Action Verbs

An **action verb** tells what someone is doing.

Rule	**Example**
▶ Words that name an action are called action verbs.	▶ We **played** in the park for two hours.

Circle the action verb in each sentence.

1. We drove for eight hours.

2. I slept for three hours.

3. Then I read a book for one hour.

4. We ate lunch at 12:00 noon.

5. At night, we walked by the lake.

UNIT 1 Sharing Stories • **Lesson 3** *The Library*

▶ **Action Verbs**

Practice

Read the paragraph below. Write an action verb in each blank.

On Saturday, we _____ to the

swimming pool. I _____ to swim.

Sometimes I _____ for pennies on

the bottom of the pool. The lifeguard

_____ me swim. I _____

to swim all day.

Proofread

Read the story below. Circle the best action verb for each sentence.

Ice hockey players **wear   have** ice skates.
They **glide   are** across the ice when they
play. The goalkeeper **has   blocks** the puck.
He must **move   be** fast. Two defenders
play   are on each side of the goalkeeper.
They **help   are** the goalkeeper.

GRAMMAR AND USAGE

Effective Beginnings and Endings

> A good beginning grabs your reader's attention. Then your reader will want to read the rest of your story.
>
> A good ending tells the reader how the story ends. It is important to have a good ending for everything you write.

This beginning can be made better. Write a better beginning on the lines.

There was a boy. He lived in the United States. He was young. His younger sister gave him a present.

_____

_____

_____

▶**Effective Beginnings and Endings**

Practice

This ending needs improvement. Write a better ending on the lines.

The gift was very special to him. He put it away in his closet. The end.

_____

_____

_____

WRITER'S CRAFT

Following Clues

Focus Sometimes a writer does not tell the reader everything. Sometimes a writer leaves clues for the reader to follow.

> ▶ Information in a story gives the reader a clue.
> ▶ Clues can help you learn more about a story's characters. For example, *Gwen put on her golden crown*. You can figure out from this sentence that Gwen is probably a queen or princess.

Identify

Read each sentence below. Then look in "Story Hour—Starring Megan!" for clues that help you know the characters better.

1. Megan really wants to learn to read. What clue tells you?

_____

2. Megan knew Andrew was there before she saw him. What clue told her?

_____

COMPREHENSION

Practice and Apply

Read the paragraphs below. Then answer
the questions.

   Megan takes Alfred for a walk every day.
When they get home, Megan feeds and waters
Alfred. Then she brushes his shiny fur. Alfred
barks his thanks.

What is Alfred? _____

What clues tell you that? _____

_____

_____

   Yesterday, Bert had trouble getting to
school on time. First he could not find his
boots. Then he could not find his mittens.
When he finally got his coat, hat, and scarf
on, the bus was waiting for him.

What is the weather like? _____

What clues tell you that? _____

_____

_____

UNIT 1 Sharing Stories • **Lesson 4** *Story Hour—Starring Megan!*

Possessive Nouns and Possessive Pronouns

Possessive words show ownership.

Rule	**Example**
▶ A **possessive noun** ends in an apostrophe *s* or just an apostrophe (').	▶ Singular: Megan**'s** mother works at the library. Plural: The girls' dresses were green.
▶ A **possessive pronoun** takes the place of a possessive noun. There is no apostrophe at the end.	▶ Singular: **Her** mother works at the library. Plural: **Their** books are over there.

Write the possessive pronoun that would replace the underlined noun.

1. Megan's brother is Nathan. _____

2. The book's cover was colorful. _____

3. He brought Andrew's book to the library. _____

4. I want to borrow Megan's and Martin's book.

_____

UNIT 1   **Sharing Stories • Lesson 4** *Story Hour—Starring Megan!*

Possessive Nouns and Possessive Pronouns

Practice

Write the possessive form of the noun at the end of each sentence.

5. _____ favorite is mystery. [Jeff]

6. I read my _____ comic books. [friend]

7. What is _____ favorite book? [you]

8. The _____ covers were torn. [books]

9. The _____ suggestion was very helpful. [librarian]

Proofread

Read the paragraph below. Change any underlined possessive pronouns that are wrong. Write the correct word above the incorrect word.

Did you like <u>mine</u> book *Runie the Unicorn*?

<u>My</u> mother's friend gave it to me for <u>mine</u>

birthday. <u>Hers</u> favorite part is when the unicorn

finds the magic crystal in the forest. <u>My</u> favorite

part is when the little girl helps the unicorn. I

didn't ruin the ending, did I?

GRAMMAR AND USAGE

UNIT 1 Sharing Stories • **Lesson 4** *Story Hour—Starring Megan!*

Staying on Topic

> You should always stay on your topic when you write. Going off the topic will confuse your reader.
>
> One way to stay on your topic is to make a plan before you write. Putting your ideas in a graphic organizer is a good way to plan.
>
> When you revise your writing, ask these questions to be sure you are staying on the topic.
>
> ▶ Did I tell my topic near the beginning of the paragraph?
>
> ▶ Do I have any details that aren't needed?

Read the sentences below. Cross out the sentences that do not stay on the topic.

Topic: Doctors help people in many ways.

1. Doctors give people medicine to cure sickness.

2. Some doctors work in hospitals.

3. Doctors can operate to heal people.

4. Doctors give shots to stop sickness.

5. Doctors and nurses work together.

► **Staying on Topic**

Practice

Write sentences that go with each topic sentence. Write the sentences on the lines.

6. Dogs make good pets.

_____

_____

_____

7. There are good reasons to play sports.

_____

_____

_____

8. There are many ways to get to school.

_____

_____

_____

WRITER'S CRAFT

UNIT 1   **Sharing Stories • Lesson 5** *Tomás and the Library Lady*

Viewpoint of a Story

Focus When a story is told by a character in the story, readers see the story through the eyes of that character. The storyteller will use words like *I* and *me*. This is called **first-person point of view.** When the story is told by someone who is not part of the story, then the storyteller uses words like *he*, *she*, and *it*. This is called **third-person point of view.**

Identify

Look at the story "Tomás and the Library Lady." What is the point

of view? _____

How do you know? _____

_____

Practice

Find your favorite book.

Title: _____

Story's point of view: _____

How do you know? _____

_____

UNIT I **Sharing Stories • Lesson 5** *Tomás and the Library Lady*

▶ **Viewpoint of a Story**

Apply

Write a short paragraph about something that happened in school from first-person point of view. Then rewrite the paragraph from third-person point of view. Perhaps you could use your teacher's viewpoint.

_____

_____

_____

_____

_____

_____

_____

_____

_____

_____

_____

COMPREHENSION

UNIT 1 Sharing Stories • **Lesson 5** *Tomas and the Library Lady*

Review

▶ Proper Nouns

Read the sentences below. Circle the proper nouns.

1. Carol and Tracie are pals.

2. They are going to Florida in December.

3. Every winter, they go to the Miami Zoo.

4. Jimmy the polar bear is always sleeping.

5. See you next Monday!

▶ Possessive Nouns and Pronouns

Correct any incorrect possessive nouns or pronouns. Write the word on the line.

6. **Mine** computer is not working! _____

7. The **computers** screen is blank. _____

8. Is **you're** computer working? _____

9. Maybe I will ask **our's** teacher to help. _____

10. We can use **hers** computer. _____

Review

GRAMMAR AND USAGE

▶ **Subject and Object Pronouns**

Underline the subject pronouns and circle the object pronouns in these sentences.

11. When will she come to visit?

12. Her letter will tell you the date.

13. It will give the time of day, also.

14. The van will meet them at the airport.

15. She will bring me a present.

▶ **Verbs**

Add an action verb to each sentence.

16. The rocket _____ off into space.

17. How long would it _____ around Earth?

18. Rockets _____ their own fuel.

19. The blast-off _____ so much noise!

20. Men, women, and dogs can _____ in space shuttles.

Drawing Conclusions

Focus Readers get ideas, or draw conclusions, about what is happening in a story by using clues from the story.

Identify

Read pages 112 and 113 of "Mushroom in the Rain." What clue lets you know that the animals are learning that they can make a little more room under the mushroom?

_____

_____

Practice

Look through "Mushroom in the Rain" to find information the writer gives about the mushroom. On the following lines, write what the information tells you about mushrooms. If you already know something about mushrooms that helps you understand how the mushroom was able to grow so big, put that information in what you write, too.

_____

_____

Name _____ Date _____

Drawing Conclusions

Apply

Read the sentences below. Then use what they tell you to draw a conclusion.

• The classes at the town's dance school are always full.

• Many people watch when the dance students perform.

• Most children in the town say they want to study dance.

• The dance school is moving to a bigger building next year.

Conclusion _____

_____

_____

_____

COMPREHENSION

UNIT 2 Kindness • **Lesson I** *Mushroom in the Rain*

Capitalization: Beginnings of Sentences

Capital letters can be used in many places. One place capital letters are used is at the beginning of a sentence.

Rule	**Example**
▶ A sentence always begins with a capital letter.	▶ Camping is fun. **Have** you ever slept outside?

Underline three times (≡) the beginning letter of each sentence.

who uses x-ray machines? doctors use x-ray machines to look inside your body. dentists also use x-ray machines to check your teeth and gums. airports use x-ray machines to check luggage for any dangerous metal objects. an x-ray machine makes a picture on a piece of film.

UNIT 2 Kindness • **Lesson 1** *Mushroom in the Rain*

Capitalization: Beginnings of Sentences

Practice

Underline three times (≡) the letters that should be capital letters in the paragraph below.

butterflies hatch as caterpillars. later, they come out of their cocoons as beautiful butterflies. butterflies come out during the day. there are about 15,000 kinds of butterflies. what is your favorite kind of butterfly?

Proofread

Underline three times (≡) the letters that should be capital letters.

Dear Butterfly,

today, I saw you flying. where were you going? you flew by yesterday at the same time! I would like to know where you were headed. maybe you were going to have your lunch. thank you for flying by and letting me see your pretty wings.

Sincerely,
A Butterfly Fan

MECHANICS

UNIT 2 Kindness • **Lesson 1** *Mushroom in the Rain*

Tone of a Personal Letter

> **Tone** tells how the writer feels about something. You should think about tone when you write.
>
> In a personal letter, the tone is usually friendly.
>
> Dear Sara,
>   How have you been? I am great. I can't wait until you visit! I'll see you soon.
>
>   Your friend,
>
>   Nicki

 **Write *friendly* next to the sentences that have a friendly tone.**

1. Thank you for the nice gift. _____

2. Don't call me again! _____

3. It is good to see you again. _____

4. You hurt my feelings. _____

5. How can I help you? _____

UNIT 2 Kindness • **Lesson I** *Mushroom in the Rain*

▶ **Tone of a Personal Letter**

Practice

Write a short letter to a friend. Be sure your letter has a friendly tone.

_____

_____

_____

_____

_____

_____

WRITER'S CRAFT

UNIT 2 Kindness • **Lesson 2** *The Elves and the Shoemaker*

Sequence

Focus Sequence is the order in which things happen in a story. The more you know about when things happen in a story, the better you can understand the story.

> Some sequence clue words tell
> ▶ the **order** in which things happen
> *first, then, finally*
> ▶ the **time** or when things happen
> *tonight, in the morning, once upon a time*

Identify

Look through "The Elves and the Shoemaker" for examples of sequence words.

1. Circle the kind of sequence words the writer uses most often.

  • time   • order

2. List four examples of sequence words or phrases from the story.

_____   _____

_____   _____

Name _____ Date _____

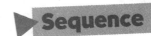

Practice and Apply

Write a story about what you did in school today. Use sequence words to tell the time and order of your story.

_____

_____

_____

_____

_____

_____

_____

COMPREHENSION

Commas: Greetings and Closings

Commas are used in different ways. One way is in friendly letters.

Rule	**Example**
▶ Write a comma after the name in the greeting of a friendly letter.	▶ Dear Cinderella,
▶ Write a comma after the closing of a friendly letter.	▶ Love, Prince Charming

Read this letter and put a comma (,) where needed.

Dear Rapunzel

 I have heard that you have the longest hair in the kingdom. Why is the prince climbing up your hair? Isn't it time you had the elevator fixed?

> Your friend
> Sleeping Beauty

Commas: Greetings and Closings

Practice

Write commas in the list of possible greetings and closings for a friendly letter.

1. Dear Oscar

2. Respectfully
Oliver

3. Best wishes
Nolah

4. My dear Nina

5. Dearest Maria

6. Love
Mario

Proofread

Add commas where they are needed. Use proofreading marks.

Dear Sleeping Beauty

   The prince only climbed up my hair once. He was in a hurry. It was an emergency. A dragon was chasing him! (We finally got the elevator fixed!)

                     Sincerely
                     Rapunzel

MECHANICS

UNIT 2   Kindness • **Lesson 2**   *The Elves and the Shoemaker*

Sentence Elaboration

Add more details to your sentences to make your writing better.

Rule	**Example**
▶ Add words that tell where or when.	▶ Dinosaurs lived a long time ago. **With details:** Many dinosaurs lived in South America over 65 million years ago.
▶ Add words that put a picture in the reader's mind.	▶ Dinosaurs were big. **With details:** Dinosaurs were giant creatures that were over 20 feet tall.
▶ Combine sentences that go together.	▶ Dinosaurs are a mystery. Scientists study fossils. **With details:** Scientists study fossils because dinosaurs are a mystery.

 **Circle the words that add detail in each sentence.**

1. The peacock had bright feathers.

2. The zoo opened in 1875 down the street.

3. The wild cheetah ran swiftly.

4. Our class went to the zoo because we were studying tigers.

UNIT 2 Kindness • **Lesson 2** *The Elves and the Shoemaker*

Sentence Elaboration

Practice

Rewrite these sentences adding details.

5. My friend is great.

_____

6. The rabbits were found.

_____

7. Adam went to Texas. His aunt lives out west.

_____

8. The men helped the family.

_____

9. Shoes are nice.

_____

WRITER'S CRAFT

Name _____ Date _____

Capitalization: Names of Days, Names of Months, and Greetings of Letters

There are several rules for capitalization. Calendars will help you remember to capitalize the days of the week and the months of the year. You must also remember to capitalize the first word of your greeting in a personal letter.

Rule	Example
▶ Days of the week begin with a capital letter.	▶ Sunday
▶ Months of the year begin with a capital letter.	▶ October
▶ Capitalize the first letter of a greeting.	▶ Dear Rolo,

Try It!

Write the name of the day or the month in each sentence below.

1. The day before Wednesday is _____.

2. New Year's Day is the first of _____.

3. The last day of the year is in _____.

4. The day before Friday is _____.

> Capitalization: Names of Days, Names of Months, and Greetings of Letters

Practice

Read this letter. Underline three times (≡) each letter that should be capitalized.

friday, may 4, 2003

dear Gretel,

 I have finally learned the number of days in the months.

 Thirty days has september,
 april, june, and november;
 All the rest have thirty-one.
 february has twenty-eight alone;
 Save in leap year, at which time,
 february's days are twenty-nine.

Love,
Hansel

Proofread

Read this letter. Underline three times (≡) letters that should be capitalized.

wednesday, november 7, 2003

dear Jimmy,

 Last october, my family went to the zoo. In november, we are going to my aunt's farm.

Sincerely,
Sam

MECHANICS

UNIT 2   Kindness • **Lesson 3** *The Paper Crane*

Structure of a Personal Letter

When you write a personal letter, make sure you have all the parts.

1. Heading
2. Greeting
3. Body
4. Closing
5. Your name

Dear Martin,
   I'm glad you could come and visit. It was great to see you. I had fun at the fair.

                              Your friend,
                              Julia

 **Try It!** **Write what part is shown on the line next to it.**

123 Main Street
Town, State 12344   _____

Dear Anne,   _____

   Thank you for coming to my party. _____
I had so much fun.

_____ Yours truly,

_____ Alice

▶ **Structure of a Personal Letter**

Practice

Write a letter to a friend or relative. Make sure you include all the parts.

_____

_____

_____

_____

_____

_____

_____

_____

                    _____

                    _____

WRITER'S CRAFT

Commas: Words in a Series

There are many places to use commas. One place they are used is in a list of things.

Rule

▶ A comma is used after each item in a series or list of things except the last one.

Example

▶ My sister went to see an ear, nose, and throat doctor.

Commas have been left out in the sentences below. Put commas where they are needed in the lists.

1. Fleas flies and bees drive me crazy!

2. Insects eat things such as wood paper and even other insects.

3. Bats birds and reptiles also eat insects.

4. What is red juicy and healthy? An apple!

Commas: Words in a Series

MECHANICS

Practice

Find each sentence that has commas in the right place. Circle the letter in front of it.

5. a. Cars can be red, blue, black, or green.
   b. Trees can be tall short, thin or wide.

6. a. The American flag is red, white, and blue.
   b. The Italian flag is red white, and green.

7. a. Bread, milk, and eggs are good for you.
   b. Bread can be white rye or, whole wheat.

8. a. Are football, basketball, and baseball, alike?
   b. Are swimming, diving, and ice skating alike?

Proofread

Read the story and add commas where they are needed. Use proofreading marks.

Flowers have soft petals pretty colors and a nice smell. To grow flowers you must plant the seeds water the plants and pull the weeds. Flowers look pretty in a garden in your office or in your house. Today, we will plant purple pansies white daisies and lilies all around the border of the garden.

Time and Order Words

You can show time in your writing by telling when things happen.

▶ Words like *today* and *next week* show time.

▶ You can show order by telling in what order things happen.

▶ Words like *first*, *next*, and *finally* show order.

Underline the time and order words in each sentence.

1. The race was yesterday.

2. It took place in the afternoon.

3. Amanda was the first to cross the finish line.

4. Last year, she came in third.

5. Pete was the second one to finish.

6. Tony was the last runner.

▶ **Time and Order Words**

Practice

Find the time and order words in the paragraph. Circle the time and order words.

Last summer, my family went camping. When we got to the campsite, we set up our tent. First, we put posts in the ground. Then, we tied ropes from the posts to the tent. Finally, we put poles in the middle of the tent to hold it up. That night, we built a fire and told stories. It was so much fun. We plan to go again next year.

WRITER'S CRAFT

UNIT 2 Kindness • **Lesson 5** *Corduroy*

Making Inferences

Focus Instead of telling you everything, writers sometimes just give you clues.

> Information in a story gives the reader a clue. Clues can help you know more about things that happen in a story.

Identify

Read page 180 of "Corduroy." Circle the sentence that is true.

• Corduroy hopes that a shopper will buy him.

• Corduroy hopes that a shopper doesn't buy him.

What clues let you know? _____

_____

Practice

Read each sentence below. Write clues from the sentence that tell what happened. Then write what that clue tells you.

1. Lin was out of breath as she told the teacher about finding someone's glasses on the playground.

Clue _____

What the clue tells you: _____

► **Making Inferences**

COMPREHENSION

2. Jacob covered his ears when he heard his brother's music playing.

Clue: _____

What the clue tells you: _____

_____

Apply

Write a paragraph about a game you like to play or a game you don't like to play without telling whether you like the game or not. Let your readers use the clues to figure out how you feel about the game.

_____

_____

_____

_____

_____

_____

_____

UNIT 2 Kindness • **Lesson 5** *Corduroy*

Quotation Marks and Underlining

Quotation marks and **underlining** are types of punctuation used in good writing.

Rule	**Example**
▶ Quotation marks are used right before and right after the words a speaker says.	▶ "There's fire in my mouth," the dragon said.
▶ Quotation marks are used around the titles of stories, poems, and book chapters.	▶ I like the story "Snow White and the Seven Dwarves."
▶ The title of a book or movie is underlined.	▶ Robert Louis Stevenson wrote <u>Treasure Island</u>.

Read the sentences below. Add quotation marks or underlining where needed.

1. The Mad Hatter said, Digital watches are best.

2. Don't eat so fast! exclaimed Little Red Riding Hood.

3. The Cat Who Became a Poet is a funny story.

MECHANICS

Practice

Write quotation marks where they belong in each sentence.

4. What's in a name? Shakespeare asked.

5. The poet Virgil said, We can't all do everything.

6. There's the very bear I've always wanted, said Goldilocks.

7. My mom said, Have a nice day!

Proofread

Underline the titles of movies or books, and put the titles of poems and stories in quotation marks.

8. My favorite book is The House at Pooh Corner.

9. Have you ever read Now We Are Six?

10. No, but now I'm reading the story Ant and the Three Little Figs.

11. My sister likes the poem Books to the Ceiling best.

Sensory Details

Descriptions make a picture in the reader's mind. Good describing words help readers see, hear, feel, smell, or taste things the writer tells them about.

▶ The sparkling, white snow was wet and cold. Don't eat the snow! It's too salty!

Circle the describing words in each sentence.

1. The kitten had soft fur.

2. We saw a large, blue, round object in the road.

3. The food tastes salty and spicy.

4. The music was loud.

5. The candle gave off a sweet smell.

▶ **Sensory Details**

Practice

Read the paragraph below. Circle the words that give sensory detail.

As I went into the movie theater, my nose filled with the smell of sweet popcorn. I could hear loud voices coming from the movies. There was happy music playing in the lobby. I sat down in the soft seat and began to eat my popcorn. It was buttery and salty. The red curtains finally opened to a huge screen. The movie was about to begin.

WRITER'S CRAFT

Name _____ Date _____

Commas: Cities, States, and Dates

You can use commas when writing names of cities and states, and in dates.

Rule	**Example**
▶ Use a comma between the city and state names in the heading of a letter.	▶ Venice, California
▶ Use a comma between the day and year when writing the date in a letter.	▶ May 31, 2003

Write commas where they belong.

1. 695 Beach Street
   Seaside California

2. April 14 1849

3. Denver Colorado

4. January 31 1984

5. 1462 Bryden Road
   Poland Ohio

Commas: Cities, States, and Dates

MECHANICS

Practice

Read this paragraph. Write commas between each day and year, and between the names of cities and states.

The train arrived in Albany New York on March 13 1997. It continued down the track until it reached Philadelphia Pennsylvania. It was sidetracked there until March 15 1997. The train finally arrived in Baltimore Maryland on March 19 1997. From there, the train brought the president home to the White House.

Proofread

Add six commas where they are needed in the paragraph below. Use proofreading marks.

My class was studying unusual names of cities in the United States. I began my report on February 6 2003. I read about Boulder Colorado. I wonder if the rocks in that city are bigger than the rocks in Little Rock Arkansas. Do buffaloes really live in Buffalo New York? Does everyone sew in Needles California? I finished my report on February 12 2003.

Structure of a Business Letter

A business letter has six parts.
1. Heading: Your address
2. Inside Address: Name and address of the person to whom you are writing; include date
3. Greeting: Usually *Dear* and the person's name to whom you are writing
4. Body: This is where you tell what you want.
5. Closing: Usually *Sincerely* or *Thank you*
6. Signature: Write your first and last name.

 **Read the letter. Label the parts.**

152 Cherry Ln. _____
Cleveland, OH 44051

Ms. Perry _____
1462 Bryden Road
Columbus, Ohio 43205
February 21, 2004

Dear Ms. Perry: _____

 The computer game I got from your company _____ didn't work. Please send me another game.

_____ Thank you,

_____ Dan Danson

UNIT 2 Kindness • **Lesson 6** *The Story of Three Whales*

Practice

Write a business letter that asks a local museum for information. Be sure to include all six parts.

_____

_____

_____

_____

_____

_____

_____

_____

_____

_____

_____

WRITER'S CRAFT

Review

▶ Capitalization

Make sure you use capital letters, commas, and punctuation marks correctly. They all help make writing clear for the reader.

Underline three times (☰) the letters in the following sentences that need to be capitalized.

1. thank-you notes thank people for things they have done.

2. last september, we visited my cousins in Maryland.

3. dear Charley,

4. on sundays, we write letters.

5. We mail them on monday.

MECHANICS

▶**Review**

▶Commas

Read the letter below. Write commas where they are needed, and underline three times the letters that should be capital letters.

sunday, november 16

dear Irina

we had such a good time at your birthday party on friday. thank you for inviting us. My sister and I liked the games the movie and the cake.

Best wishes
Lana

▶Punctuation

Read the invitation below. Insert two pairs of quotation marks. Underline two movie titles, and underline three times two letters that should be capitalized.

Movie Show
saturday, october 25
2:00 p.m.
Dru and Sue say, Come one, come all!
Special movie showing of
Cinderella in Space and
Prince Charming Goes to Mars
Call us at 432–1865 and say Yes!

Background Information

Tell your reader facts about a person, place, or event. This will help your reader better understand what you want to say.

▶ I like my new school better than my old school.
With background information: I like my new school better than my old school because my old school didn't have a tennis team.

 **Underline the background information in each sentence.**

1. It is amazing my dog can run so well. He got hit by a car two months ago.

2. The day I didn't get picked for the football team was a good day. I ended up trying out for the baseball team and I made it!

3. My sister is very smart. She can read. She is three years old.

4. My grandma's dark, dusty attic is a great place. It has old boxes filled with treasures.

5. The ski trip was fun. We skied down a huge mountain, then we drank hot chocolate.

UNIT 2 Kindness • **Lesson 7** *Cinderella*

▶ Background Information

Practice

Give background information about these topics.

6. Second grade is better than first grade.

_____

_____

_____

7. My last school trip was fun.

_____

_____

_____

8. My family lives downtown.

_____

_____

_____

WRITER'S CRAFT

UNIT 3 Look Again • **Lesson 1** *I See Animals Hiding*

Kinds of Sentences

There are different kinds of sentences.

Rule	**Example**
▶A **declarative sentence** makes a statement. It always ends with a period (.).	▶Mars is a planet.
▶An **interrogative sentence** asks a question. It always ends in a question mark (?).	▶Will people ever live on Mars?
▶An **imperative sentence** gives directions or a command. It always ends in a period (.).	▶Begin the countdown now.
▶An **exclamatory sentence** shows strong feelings. It always ends with an exclamation mark (!).	▶What a perfect launch!

Read each sentence below. Write the type of sentence on the line.

1. Go outside and build a snowman. _____

2. Then, mother said, "Wear your cap, Stan!" _____

▶ **Kinds of Sentences**

Practice

Put the correct end mark at the end of each sentence.

1. Where does snow come from

2. Icy droplets of water in clouds turn into snowflakes

3. It's amazing that no two snowflakes are alike

4. Where do the water droplets come from

5. They come from Earth's lakes, rivers, and oceans

Proofread

Read the paragraph below. Insert end marks where they belong. Use proofreading marks.

What can change in a minute or stay the same for months at a time The weather The tropics are hot areas of the world In the tropics, the weather doesn't change for months at a time In some parts of the world, storms can change a sunny day into a rainy day Trying to figure out what the weather will be is a difficult job

UNIT 3 Look Again • **Lesson I** *I See Animals Hiding*

Organizing Expository Writing

> ▶ Expository writing gives facts. Expository writing is not make-believe.
>
> ▶ Start your expository paragraph with your topic. Then add details. End with a sentence that sums up your main points.
>
> Here are some tips to organize your details:
> ▶ Put the most important facts first.
> ▶ List in the order in which things happen.

 **Read these statements. Write *true* if the statement is true. Write *make-believe* if the statement is make-believe.**

1. The firefighters put out the fire.

_____

2. My dog called the fire department.

_____

3. The family woke up to the smoke alarms.

_____

4. All of the aliens were safe.

_____

▶ **Organizing Expository Writing**

Practice

**Make a list of the things you do in a
normal day at school.**

_____

_____

_____

_____

WRITER'S CRAFT

Topic Sentences

A topic sentence tells the main idea of a paragraph. It is often the first sentence of a paragraph.

Topic Sentence: Exercise will change your life for the better.
This sentence tells the reader that the paragraph is going to be about exercise and how it will change your life.

 **Try It!** **Read the sentences below. Circle the topic sentence.**

1. Robinson was a major league baseball player.

2. He played for the Brooklyn Dodgers in 1946.

3. Jackie Robinson made history.

UNIT 3 Look Again • **Lesson I** *I See Animals Hiding*

▶**Topic Sentences**

Practice

Write a topic sentence for this paragraph.

_____

I learned about insects there. I also got a lot of
exercise. I swam and hiked. I met some great
new friends. I can't wait to go back to camp
next summer.

**Think about something you like to do or
study. Write a topic sentence about it.**

_____

_____

_____

WRITER'S CRAFT

Drawing Conclusions

Focus Thinking about the information in a story can help readers make decisions about what is happening.

> Readers can **draw conclusions** about a character or event in a story by using information in the story's words and pictures.

Identify

Read these sentences from "They Thought They Saw Him." Write the conclusion you can make from the underlined information in each sentence.

1. <u>All winter</u> little dark chameleon had lived, <u>safe and asleep</u>, beneath the granary where the people kept their seed corn.

_____

_____

2. As he moved on <u>quick silent feet</u>, he began to forget the sleepy winter dark and felt the joy in the first wakeful light of spring.

_____

_____

UNIT 3 Look Again • **Lesson 2** *They Thought They Saw Him*

Drawing Conclusions

COMPREHENSION

Practice and Apply

Read the following paragraph. Then answer the questions below by drawing conclusions.

Our teacher, Ms. Smith, began talking to herself. "Now, where are they? I can't read without them." She looked through her desk drawers. She looked in her purse. She patted her pockets. As Ms. Smith scratched her head, we began to giggle. She found what she had been looking for. "I always leave them up there," she laughed.

What was Ms. Smith doing?

_____

_____

Why did the students giggle when Ms. Smith scratched her head?

_____

_____

UNIT 3 Look Again • **Lesson 2** *They Thought They Saw Him*

Linking Verbs and Helping Verbs

Sometimes verbs don't show action. These verbs are called linking and helping verbs.

Rule	**Example**
▶ A **linking verb** joins, or connects, the parts of a sentence to make it complete.	▶ There **is** a pretty shell on the beach.
▶ A **helping verb** helps the main verb in a sentence tell when something will happen, has happened, or is happening.	▶ We **are** planning to look for shells tomorrow.

Read each sentence. Write an *L* if the underlined verb is a linking verb. Write an *H* if the verb is a helping verb.

1. I <u>was</u> swimming like a fish today. _____

2. Fish <u>have been</u> swimming in the oceans for

millions of years. _____

3. The fish <u>was</u> cold. _____

► **Linking Verbs and Helping Verbs**

Practice

Read the paragraph below. Underline the linking verbs. Circle the helping verbs.

There are more than 20,000 types of fish. I have eaten swordfish and sardines. Have you ever eaten eel? A shark is a very big fish. Are sea horses fish? The lionfish is orange.

Proofread

Read the paragraph below. Write in linking or helping verbs to complete the sentences.

There _____ six fish in my aquarium.

The blue fish _____ swimming faster

than the orange fish. My cat _____

watching them swim. I _____ tried

to teach the cat to behave. These fish

_____ not for dinner, Miss Kitty!

GRAMMAR AND USAGE

Note Taking

Taking good notes helps you remember facts. These facts can help you write a good report. Remembering facts also helps you do well on tests.

Remember these tips to take good notes:
▶ Use a different page for each kind of information you collect.
▶ Make a heading for each kind of information. You may have many facts under one heading.
▶ Write your notes in your own words.
▶ Write down only the most important facts.
▶ Write neatly.

 **Look at the topic below. Write some notes about things you know about it.**

The Moon

_____

_____

_____

_____

_____

▶ **Note Taking**

WRITER'S CRAFT

Practice

Read the paragraph below. Take notes on the information you read.

Earth is very interesting. It is made mostly of water. There are also forests and mountains on Earth's surface. It is 93 million miles from the sun, but we still feel the sun's heat. Earth takes one year to revolve around the sun. It rotates on its axis in one day.

<u>Earth</u>

_____

_____

_____

_____

UNIT 3 Look Again • **Lesson 3** *Hungry Little Hare*

Subject-Verb Agreement

A sentence has a subject and a verb that agree. This means that the subject and the verb must both be singular, or they must both be plural.

Rule	**Example**
▶If the subject of a sentence is singular, the verb must be singular.	▶A **plant needs** air, sunlight, and water.
▶If the subject of a sentence is plural, the verb must be plural.	▶**Plants need** warmth to grow.

Try It!

Write *S* if the sentence has a singular subject and verb and *P* if the sentence has a plural subject and verb.

1. A house plant grows indoors. _____

2. Herbs are plants used in cooking. _____

3. Wildflowers grow by themselves outside. _____

4. An evergreen tree keeps its leaves all year

long. _____

Subject-Verb Agreement

Practice

Write *am*, *is*, or *are* to agree with the subject in each sentence.

5. We _____ learning about plants and trees.

6. A tree _____ a wooded plant.

Write *have* or *has* to agree with the subject in each sentence.

7. Evergreens _____ leaves or needles.

8. The desert _____ many plants.

Proofread

Read the following sentences. Choose the verb in parentheses that correctly completes each sentence.

9. Leaves _____ color in the fall. (change, changes)

10. A cactus plant _____ spines, but no leaves. (has, have)

GRAMMAR AND USAGE

UNIT 3 Look Again • **Lesson 3** *Hungry Little Hare*

Transition Words

> **Transition words** help your sentences go together smoothly. Time and order words are examples of transition words.
>
> Here are some transition words:
> first   next   then
> last   later   finally   in the beginning

 **Underline the transition words in each sentence.**

1. I cleared the table. Then, my sister washed the dishes.

2. In the beginning, I liked math class.

3. First, I washed my face.

4. Then, I brushed my teeth.

5. Finally, I brushed my hair.

Transition Words

Practice

Find the transition words in the paragraph. Write them on the lines.

It was time to get ready for the party. I swept the house; meanwhile, Mom put up decorations. Next, we put icing on the cake. Then, Dad made sandwiches. Later, we got the games ready. Finally, we were ready for the party.

_____

_____

WRITER'S CRAFT

Parts of a Sentence

A sentence is a group of words that expresses a complete thought. A sentence has two parts: a naming part and a telling part.

Rule	**Example**
▶ The **subject** of a sentence includes all the words in the naming part.	▶ **Subject** The game of soccer
▶ The **predicate** includes all the words in the telling part.	▶ **Predicate** is played around the world.

 **Try It!**

Underline the subject once and underline the predicate twice in each sentence.

1. Soccer began in England in the 1800s.

2. Two teams of 11 players each compete in soccer.

3. The players try to put a ball into the other team's goal.

4. The goals are two nets at opposite ends of a rectangular field.

► **Parts of a Sentence**

GRAMMAR AND USAGE

Practice

Write an *S* if the underlined part is a subject, and write a *P* if it is a predicate. Put an *S* or *P* on the line after the sentence.

5. The game of rugby uses an oval-shaped ball. _____

6. The players on a rugby team carry, kick, or

   pass the ball. _____

7. Fifteen players make up a team. _____

8. The object of the game is to score goals. _____

Proofread

Read the sentences below. Underline the subject once. Underline the predicate twice.

9. The team with the ball is the offensive team.

10. The game of football developed from the English game of rugby.

11. The team trying to stop the offensive team is the defensive team.

Organizing Expository Writing

> ▶ Expository writing gives facts. It tells something true about a subject.
> ▶ Start your expository paragraph with your topic. Then add details. End with a sentence that sums up your main points.
>
> Here are some tips to organize your details:
> ▶ Put the most important facts first.
> ▶ List in the order in which things happen. This can be the events of a day or steps to a recipe.

Number these details in order of importance.

Topic: Doctors

_____ They go to school for many years.

_____ They help people feel better.

_____ They save lives.

_____ They work in offices and hospitals.

UNIT 3 Look Again • **Lesson 4** *How to Hide an Octopus*

Organizing Expository Writing

Practice

Write a paragraph based on the facts from this story. Be sure to put the facts in order.

▶ She got a call Saturday afternoon.

▶ Her family put the posters up all over town.

▶ Her dog was found!

▶ Her dog was finally home.

▶ Emma lost her dog.

▶ Her family made posters with her dog's picture and their phone number.

_____

_____

_____

_____

_____

_____

WRITER'S CRAFT

Supporting Details

> ▶ A **main idea** is the topic of the paragraph.
> ▶ **Supporting details** tell about the main idea.
>
> Main Idea: Farming is hard work.
> Supporting Details:
> ▶ You have to feed the animals.
> ▶ Some farmers plant and harvest.
> ▶ Other farmers milk the cows and do other chores.

 **Read the main ideas below. Then cross out one sentence that is not a supporting detail.**

Main Idea: Moira is in charge of the costumes for the class play.

Details: Moira found some long dresses in her mother's closet.

She likes to go to plays.

She added feathers and buttons to the dresses.

They were perfect for the ballroom scene in the play at school.

UNIT 3 Look Again • **Lesson 4** *How to Hide an Octopus*

Supporting Details

Practice

Write three supporting details about the topic below.

Topic: Weekends are fun.

_____

_____

_____

WRITER'S CRAFT

Classify and Categorize

Focus **Classifying and categorizing** means putting things into groups. Classifying can help readers keep track of information in a story.

> To classify information
> ▶ name the categories for things, characters, or events
> ▶ list the things, characters, or events that fit under each category
> ▶ sometimes things, characters, or events can fit into more than one category

Identify

The characters in "How the Guinea Fowl Got Her Spots" can be classified in a number of different ways. Look at the categories listed below and write the animals that fit under each.

Friends: _____

Large animals: _____

Small animals: _____

Four-legged animals: _____

Name _____ Date _____

▶ Classify and Categorize

Practice

Look at the list of things below. List each thing under the correct category. Remember, some things can fit in more than one category.

cutting board	scissors	board
sponge eraser	paper	can opener

Things that are useful in a school classroom

_____

_____

_____

_____

Things that are useful in a kitchen

_____

_____

_____

_____

Apply

Make a list of other things that would fit into each of the categories.

School classroom: _____

_____

Kitchen: _____

_____

COMPREHENSION

Complete Sentences

A **complete sentence** has a subject and a predicate.
A **run-on sentence** is two ideas mixed together.
A **sentence fragment** is missing a subject or predicate.

Rule	Example
	Run-on
▶ To correct a run-on sentence, write two sentences.	▶ The fog covers the bridge it stands over the water.
	Correct
	The fog covers the bridge. It stands over the water.
	Fragment
▶ To correct a sentence fragment, add the missing subject or predicate to the sentence.	▶ Over one billion vehicles
	Correct
	Over one billion vehicles have crossed the bridge.

Write *F* for fragment or *R* for run-on.

1. Orange trees plenty of water. _____

2. Potatoes grow in cool climates they can't

   grow in freezing weather. _____

▶ **Complete Sentences**

GRAMMAR AND USAGE

Practice

Circle the word group that correctly completes each sentence.

3. The first bridges   **were tree trunks.**
   some footbridges.

4. Pontoon bridges   **the surface.**
   float on the water.

5. Arches   **are very strong.**
   curved supports.

Proofread

Read the paragraph below. Correct the run-on sentences. Write in end marks and underline three (≡) times the letters that should be capitalized.

A map has arrows that show directions the main directions are north, south, east, and west. There are also directions between the four main directions. The direction between north and east is called northeast southeast is between south and east. Between west and north is called northwest, and between west and south is called southwest.

UNIT 3 Look Again • **Lesson 5** *How the Guinea Fowl Got Her Spots*

Place and Location Words

> ▶ Place and location words tell where something is.
>
> Some place and location words are:
>
> | | | | |
> |---|---|---|---|
> | above | over | in front of | next to |
> | on top of | below | beneath | under |
> | near | inside | outside | beside |

 **Look around your classroom and answer these questions. Use place and location words from the box.**

1. Where is your teacher's desk?

_____

2. Where is the pencil sharpener?

_____

3. Where are your books?

_____

4. Where is your coat?

_____

▶ **Place and Location Words**

Practice

Finish these sentences about things in your bedroom.

5. _____ is on top of
   the bed.

6. _____ is beneath
   the bed.

7. _____ is beside
   the bed.

8. _____ is on top of
   the dresser.

9. _____ is in front
   of the dresser.

WRITER'S CRAFT

Main Idea

Focus The **main idea** tells what a paragraph is mostly about.

▸ A **main-idea sentence** gives the main idea of a paragraph. The other sentences in a paragraph give details or information about the main idea.

▸ A main-idea sentence often comes **first** in a paragraph. Placing the main idea sentence first helps readers know what the paragraph is about.

Identify

Look through "Animal Camouflage" for main-idea sentences. Write one main-idea sentence below. Then give some details about the main idea.

Page: _____

Main idea: _____

_____

Details about the main idea: _____

_____

_____

UNIT 3 Look Again • **Lesson 6** *Animal Camouflage*

▶Review

▶ Parts of a Sentence

Underline the subject once and underline the predicate twice.

9. Pumas are members of the cat family.

10. A puma can live in a hot area or in a forest.

11. The mountain lion is another name for the puma.

12. Pumas have sharp teeth.

13. A puma's speed helps it stay alive.

▶ Complete Sentences

Write *F* for fragment, *R* for run-on, or *C* for complete sentence after each of the following groups of words.

14. White light contains all the colors of the rainbow. ____

15. A flower's colors bees. ____

16. Squirrels are color-blind guinea pigs are, too. ____

17. Red shoes in blue light. ____

GRAMMAR AND USAGE

Fact and Opinion

A **fact** can be checked and proven to be true. An **opinion** cannot be proven. It is a person's idea or feeling.

▶ Fact: Germany is in Europe.
▶ Opinion: Germany is a nice place to visit.

Read each sentence. Write *F* for fact or *O* for opinion.

1. _____ My mother is the best lawyer in the world.

2. _____ Tomorrow we have gym in the afternoon.

3. _____ Mushrooms grow in the ground.

4. _____ My friend has the nicest bike.

5. _____ Trenton is the capital of New Jersey.

▶**Fact and Opinion**

WRITER'S CRAFT

{ **Practice** }

Read the following facts. Then change the fact to an opinion. The first one is done for you.

6. Fact: There are many breeds of rabbits.

Opinion: <u>White rabbits are the best breed.</u>

7. Fact: There are fifty states in the United States.

Opinion: _____

8. Fact: Marshmallows are made with sugar.

Opinion: _____

9. Fact: Trees give off oxygen.

Opinion: _____

10. Fact: Florida has many beaches.

Opinion: _____

Adjectives

Adjectives make writing more interesting. Forming a picture in your mind of the objects you want to describe will help you find the right adjectives.

Rule

▶ An **adjective** is a word that describes a noun. An adjective tells *how much, how many,* or *what kind.*

▶ **Articles** are special kinds of adjectives. There are three articles: *a, an,* and *the.*

Example

▶ There are **five** classes of **living** things.

▶ **An** insect or **a** bird might be included in **the** animal class.

Read the poem below. Circle the adjectives and articles.

For a big green plant
Or a tiny little ant
Resting in the woods is nice.
Each living thing must
Share cool shade and just
Take a break in paradise.

UNIT 4 Fossils • **Lesson 3** *Dinosaur Fossils*

▶ Classify and Categorize

Practice

Make a list for each category below.

Things I like to do   **Things I don't like to do**

Apply

Look at each item below. Think of two categories to sort these items into and write them in the box. Then sort the items under the two categories.

| subways | tractors | barns | skyscrapers |
| fields | many people | | |

COMPREHENSION

UNIT 4 Fossils • **Lesson 3** *Dinosaur Fossils*

Linking and Helping Verb Tenses

Finding the right verb and using the right tense of the verb is important in both speaking and writing. You can make your writing better by using the proper tense.

Rule

▶A **present tense** linking or helping verb tells about something that is happening now.

▶A **past tense** linking or helping verb tells about something that happened in the past.

Example

▶The Nile River **is** the longest river in the world.

▶The Nile River **was** important to the people in Egypt.

 **Try It!**

Underline the past tense verbs.

1. Louis Braille was a teacher.

2. He was blinded at the age of three.

3. In school, he could not read or write.

4. Then, he was sent to a school in Paris.

UNIT 4 Fossils • **Lesson 3** *Dinosaur Fossils*

▶ **Linking and Helping Verb Tenses**

Practice

Write the correct verb in the space in each sentence.

5. France _____ a country in Europe.

6. The area _____ ruled by the Romans.

7. We _____ studying French history.

8. Yesterday we _____ singing songs.

9. Today we _____ painting pictures.

Proofread

Read the sentences below and find the mistakes. Cross out the incorrect verb and write the correct one above it.

Once I was riding a horse in a desert. My horse am running very fast. We is trying to reach a town. The town are very far away. When the moon have risen in the sky, we saw the friendly town! The people there was very friendly.

GRAMMAR AND USAGE

UNIT 4 Fossils • **Lesson 3** *Dinosaur Fossils*

Figurative Language

Figurative language is a word or group of words that stand for more than their real meanings. They are used to create pictures in a reader's mind.

Figures of Speech

▶ A **simile** compares two things by using the word *like* or *as*.

▶ A **metaphor** compares two things without using the word *like* or *as*.

▶ **Personification** gives an object human qualities.

▶ The rabbit's fur was **like** a blanket of soft snow.

▶ The rabbit's fur **was** a blanket of soft snow.

▶ The car **coughed** and **wheezed** as it tried to start.

 **After each sentence, write *S* if it has a simile, *M* if it has a metaphor, and *P* if it has personification.**

1. Adam's eyes were big saucers. _____

2. Susan fell like a rock. _____

3. The kite was a bird flying in the sky. _____

4. The tree danced in the wind. _____

5. His bag was as heavy as a brick. _____

Name _____ Date _____

▶ **Figurative Language**

Practice

Compare these things by writing a word to finish each sentence.

1. The cereal tasted like

2. I ran as fast as

3. The banana felt like

4. These shoes are as big as

5. The kitchen smells like

WRITER'S CRAFT

Nouns: Singular and Plural

Nouns can be **singular** or **plural**.

Rule	**Example**
▶A singular noun names one.	▶star animal plant idea
▶Plural nouns name more than one.	▶stars animals plants ideas
▶Most nouns add -*s* to form the plural form.	▶cars bikes trains
▶Some nouns add -*es* to words ending in *s*, *x*, *z*, *ss*, *ch*, or *sh*.	▶brush brushes box boxes
▶Other nouns ending in *y* change the *y* to -*i* and add -*es*.	▶buddy buddies
▶There are some special nouns. These nouns change when they are made plural.	▶wolf wolves

Try It!

Circle the plural nouns and underline the singular nouns in the sentences below.

1. Some parts of the world are always hot.

2. At the equator, climates are hot and rainy.

UNIT 4 Fossils • **Lesson 4** *Why Did the Dinosaurs Disappear?*

▶ **Nouns: Singular and Plural**

Practice

Write the plural form of each noun below.

3. ax _____

4. rocket _____

5. hat _____

6. man _____

7. sky _____

Proofread

Find the mistakes in the paragraph below. Cross out the incorrect word, and write the correct form of the word above it.

One-fifth of Earth is covered with deserts.

Deserts have only a few plantes and animales.

No cloudes can form in deserts, because there

is not much rain. There are a lot of sand dunes.

Cameles and snakees can live in deserts also.

GRAMMAR AND USAGE

Name _____ Date _____

Organizing Descriptive Writing

▶ **Descriptions** are words that make a picture in the reader's mind.

▶ Start your descriptive paragraph with your topic. Then add details that make a picture in the reader's mind. End with a sentence that sums up your main points.

 **Write a descriptive sentence about each topic. Be sure to use describing words.**

1. Topic: Your best friend

_____

2. Topic: Your pet or favorite animal

_____

3. Topic: Your school

_____

▶ **Organizing Descriptive Writing**

Practice

Write a paragraph describing your house.
Write details about how things look, feel,
smell, and sound.

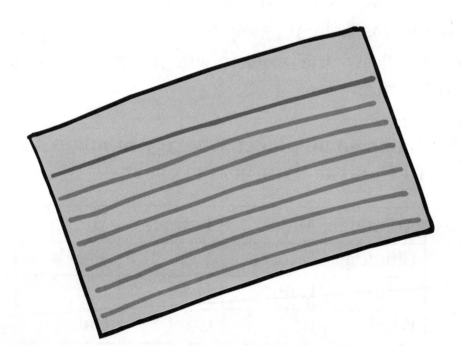

WRITER'S CRAFT

UNIT 4 Fossils • **Lesson 4** *Why Did the Dinosaurs Disappear?*

Collecting and Organizing Data

Data is information about something. There are many places to collect data. You have to know where to look. Some places to find information:

▶ An **atlas** is a book of maps.

▶ A **dictionary** lists words in ABC order. You can find a word's spelling and meaning.

▶ An **encyclopedia** has facts on many subjects.

▶ **Magazines** and **newspapers** have many up-to-date facts.

▶ You can also get information from a **museum** or **zoo.**

Organize data in a way that makes sense.

Ways to organize your data:

▶ A **chart** is a box that has rows and columns. Words are written in boxes to help readers find information quickly.

▶ A **time line** shows the order in which events happen over a period of time.

 **Name some places where you might look to find the data in this chart.**

Animal	Male	Female	Young
Chicken	Rooster	Hen	Chick
Rabbit	Buck	Doe	Bunny
Whale	Bull	Cow	Calf

UNIT 4   Fossils • **Lesson 4**   *Why Did the Dinosaurs Disappear?*

▶**Collecting and Organizing Data**

Practice

Tell where you might find data about these topics.

1. Places in South Africa

2. The latest news

3. The meanings of words

4. Jupiter

5. Dinosaurs

WRITER'S CRAFT

Sequence

Focus Sequence is the order of what happens in a story. Writers often use **time and order words** to help readers follow the sequence.

Time and order words show

▶ the **order** in which events happen. Words such as *first, then, so, when,* and *finally* show order.

▶ the passage of **time** in a story. Words such as *winter, today,* and *night* show time.

Identify

Look through "Monster Tracks." Find sentences with time and order words. Write the page numbers and the words. Write *T* next to the word if it shows time and *O* if it shows order.

1. Page: Word:

2. Page: Word:

3. Page: Word:

4. Page: Word:

5. Page: Word:

▶ **Sequence**

COMPREHENSION

Practice

Read the paragraph below. Fill in the spaces with words that show time.

_____ my sister and I made dinner

for our friends. We invited them to come over

_____ . _____ we are

going to invite our cousins, too.

In the paragraph below, fill in the spaces with words that show order.

The _____ step in making scrambled eggs is to mix eggs with milk, salt, and pepper.

_____ pouring the eggs in the pan,

melt butter in the pan. _____ pour the eggs and milk into the pan.

_____ cook 3 to 4 minutes.

Apply

Write two sentences about what you did yesterday. Use time and order words.

_____

_____

Adverbs

Adverbs make writing more clear and more descriptive. You can make your verbs stronger with adverbs.

Rule	**Example**
▶ An adverb describes a verb and tells *how*, *when*, or *where*.	▶ The bones in your body grow **fast.** I went to the store **yesterday.** Stay **here** and drink your milk.

Read the sentences. Circle the adverbs.

1. Your muscles let you move easily.

2. Cardiac muscle keeps your heart beating strongly.

3. Skeletal muscles let us move our bones slowly.

4. You can usually control your skeletal muscles.

5. Nerve signals from the brain always tell the muscles what to do.

UNIT 4 Fossils • **Lesson 5** *Monster Tracks*

▶**Adverbs**

GRAMMAR AND USAGE

Practice

Read the sentences below. Write an adverb in the blank that best completes the sentence.

6. The cheetah can run _____.

7. They _____ stretch their arms and legs.

8. Some cheetahs swim _____.

9. A cheetah can growl _____.

10. Baby cheetahs _____ stay close to their mothers.

Proofread

Read the paragraph below. Circle the adverbs.

    Ants and termites live in large colonies. Ants have long legs and can run swiftly. They can climb anywhere. Termites eat mostly plants. Many termites build mounds underground. The mounds have thick walls to keep out anteaters. Ants can easily lift things that weigh more than they do. Army ants are always on the move. The queen waits patiently for the workers to bring her food. Studying insects is sometimes fun.

UNIT 4 Fossils • **Lesson 5** *Monster Tracks*

Paragraph Form

Rules for Writing Paragraphs:

1. Begin a paragraph on a new line.
2. Indent the first line of each paragraph.
3. Write a topic sentence at the beginning of the paragraph that tells the main idea.
4. Write sentences that support the main idea.
5. Begin a new paragraph for each new idea.

 **Tell what is missing from this paragraph.**

There are over 400 species of them. They live in the ocean. Their fins and tails help them to swim fast. They eat other, smaller fish. The great white is the largest type of shark. It is about 15 feet long. Sharks are interesting fish.

Practice

Write a paragraph telling about your favorite holiday. Make sure you include all the parts in your paragraph.

WRITER'S CRAFT

Review

▶ Adjectives and Adverbs

Read the sentences below. Circle the adjectives and underline the adverbs in each sentence.

1. Gems are stones used to make pretty jewelry.

2. Gemstones are often found at the bottom of rivers.

3. Diamond is a hard material.

▶ Contractions

Form contractions from the boldfaced words in each sentence.

4. Rocks on Earth's surface **do not** last

   forever. _____

5. They **cannot** withstand the effects of rain

   and wind. _____

6. These rocks **are not** very old. _____

7. You **would not** want to eat those minerals.

_____

GRAMMAR AND USAGE

▶**Review**

▶ **Linking and Helping Verb Tenses**

Look at the words in boldface. Write a *pr* if the verb is present tense and a *pt* if the verb is past tense.

8. These mountains **were formed** in the Ice Age. _____

9. These pies **are** not pumpkin. _____

10. This picture **was taken** 50 years ago. _____

11. My grandmother **was** 50 last year. _____

12. Who **is helping** with the decorations? _____

▶ **Nouns: Singular and Plural**

Write the plural or singular form of the boldfaced noun on the line at the end of each sentence.

13. The lioness has one **baby.** _____

14. Autumn is the time to rake all the **leaves** in

the yard. _____

15. The **boys** are better at yard work. _____

16. Does your city have more than one **library?** _____

17. Please put this book back on the **shelf.** _____

Topic Sentences

Rule	Example
▶ A topic sentence tells the main idea of the paragraph. It is often the first sentence of a paragraph.	▶ **Topic Sentence:** Painting is fun. This sentence tells the reader the paragraph is about painting.

 **Circle the topic sentence.**

1. It is the highest mountain in Japan.

2. The view from the top is amazing.

3. It is 12,388 feet tall.

4. Mt. Fuji is Japan's most popular place to visit.

5. It is a breathtaking sight.

▶ **Topic Sentences**

(**Practice**)

Write a topic sentence for this paragraph.

    It is a brass instrument that is hollow inside. It makes sounds when air is blown into the cup-shaped mouthpiece. It has a fancy design. The French horn has been around for many years.

Write a topic sentence about your favorite instrument.

WRITER'S CRAFT

UNIT 5 Courage • **Lesson I** *Molly the Brave and Me*

Point of View

Focus **Point of view** is how the author decides to tell the story. He or she can tell it through a character or through someone outside of the story.

When a story is told from the **first-person point of view**
▶ the storyteller is a character in the story
▶ the clue words *I*, *my*, *mine*, *us*, *our*, and *we* are used

When a story is told from the **third-person point of view**
▶ the storyteller is not a character in the story
▶ the clue words *she*, *he*, *her*, *they*, and *their* are used

Identify

Read page 123 of "Molly the Brave and Me" for clue words that show who is telling the story. Write the clue words and the name of the character telling the story.

Clue words: _____

Who is telling the story? _____

UNIT 5 Courage • **Lesson I** *Molly the Brave and Me*

▶ **Point of View**

Find an example in which the storyteller shares her own thoughts or feelings. Write the first three or four words of the example. Share your example with your classmates.

Page: _____ Example: _____

_____

Practice

Circle each word that gives a clue about the point of view.

1. Marsha and her mother almost missed the plane. They had a hard time getting a taxi to the airport. Luckily, their plane was late taking off.

2. Jamie and I shared our snacks. Dad gave us apples, sandwiches, and peanuts. We ate the snacks at the picnic table.

Apply

Write about something you and a friend did together. Write using first-person point of view.

_____

_____

_____

COMPREHENSION

UNIT 5 Courage • **Lesson 1** *Molly the Brave and Me*

Capitalization: I and Proper Nouns

There are many places to use capital letters. Use them in proper nouns.

Rule	**Example**
▶ The word *I* is always written as a capital letter.	▶ My brother and **I** took a boat trip down the river.
▶ A proper noun names a particular person, place, or thing. A proper noun always begins with a capital letter.	▶ The **Nile River** is longer than the **Tigris River**.

Read the sentences below. Circle the proper nouns in the sentences below that should be capitalized.

1. The third president of the united states was thomas jefferson.

2. Jefferson was born in virginia.

3. In 1776, jefferson wrote the declaration of independence.

UNIT 5 Courage • **Lesson I** *Molly the Brave and Me*

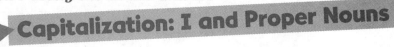

Capitalization: I and Proper Nouns

MECHANICS

Practice

Circle the word with the correct capital letters.

4. Maria   maria   and I are going to study Lewis and Clark.

5. We learned that they went west of the **missouri river   Missouri River.**

6. i   I   read that they reached the Pacific Ocean.

7. Sacajawea was a   **Native American native american**   that guided the explorers.

Proofread

Underline three times (☰) each letter in the paragraph below that should be a capital letter.

Last saturday, i saw a white tiger at the San Diego Zoo. He sat alone as my uncle john and i watched him. The african Safari area is my favorite place. The big gorilla named bob is always funny to see.

Organizing Narrative Writing

> ▶ **Narrative writing** tells a story.
>
> ▶ Narrative writing has three parts: Characters, Plot, and Setting.
>
> ▶ A narrative can be a real story, like something that happened to you or a friend.
>
> ▶ A narrative can also be a made-up story, like a fairy tale.
>
> ▶ Always try to have an exciting beginning and ending.

**Think of a story that you would like to tell.
List the characters on the lines.**

Characters

_____

_____

_____

►**Organizing Narrative Writing**

Practice

Think about your story. Write a sentence or two describing your plot.

Plot

_____

_____

_____

Where is your story going to take place? Write a list of adjectives that describe your story's setting.

Setting

_____

_____

_____

WRITER'S CRAFT

UNIT 5 Courage • **Lesson 2** *Dragons and Giants*

Conjunctions and Interjections

Conjunctions and **interjections** are special words. Use them to make writing easier or more interesting to read.

Rule	**Example**
▶A **conjunction** is a word that connects words or ideas.	▶Ziggy **and** I are going to the zoo. We will go today **or** tomorrow.
▶An **interjection** is a word that shows strong feelings. It is followed by an exclamation point.	▶**Yes!** I would love to come to your party. **No!** I won't bring my little brother.

 **Try It!**

Read the sentences. Circle the conjunctions. Underline the interjections.

1. My sister read a story to my brother and me.

2. Oh! Alice just fell down into a big hole.

3. She was following a rabbit, or was it a hare?

4. Goodness! She fell down and hurt her knee.

MECHANICS

Conjunctions and Interjections

Practice

Read the sentences. Write *and*, *or*, or *but* to complete each sentence.

5. Mom _____ I are going to walk to school by ourselves today.

6. We will walk, _____ we may run.

7. We may even skip, _____ we won't be late for school.

8. Mom is wearing a blue coat _____ a green hat.

9. I am wearing a red jacket, _____ I am wearing a red cap today.

Proofread

Read the following story. Add an exclamation mark after the interjections.

The sidewalks and the streets were slippery with snow. Oh, no How would I get to school safely today? I bundled myself up in my coat and my hat. Oops I almost forgot my gloves. Now I'm finally ready to go. The steps at school are spread with salt.Wow This is easy.

A story's **plot** is made up of the things that happen in the story.
▶ A plot has a beginning, middle, and end.
▶ The characters have a problem. The problem is solved at the end of the story.
▶ Usually ends with a climax, or high point, of the story and a solution to the problem.

**Look at the story "Dragons and Giants."
Look for the main characters, plot, and
setting. List below.**

Characters: _____

_____

Setting: _____

_____

Problem: _____

_____

▶Plot

Practice

Write about the story "Dragons and Giants." Be sure to tell about the plot.

WRITER'S CRAFT

Suspense and Surprise

> ▶ **Suspense** makes the reader want to find out what happens next.
>
> ▶ **Surprise** is when something happens that the reader didn't expect.

Read each paragraph. Circle the letter of the paragraph that has suspense.

A. It was a rainy, windy night. There was a loud noise at the door. I opened the door. There was no one there. My dog came out from behind the steps. He was all wet and shaking. He had scared me. I'd forgotten I had left him outside.

B. It was a dark and stormy night. Suddenly, I heard a strange noise. It came from the front door. Again and again, I heard the same sound. What could make such a sound? I had to know. I took a deep breath and flung open the door. I jumped! As I breathed a sigh of relief, my dog came out from behind the steps. He was trembling and soaked. I had left him out in the rain!

UNIT 5 Courage • **Lesson 2** *Dragons and Giants*

Suspense and Surprise

Practice

Write a paragraph about an ordinary afternoon in your school's library. Plan a surprise ending.

_____

_____

_____

_____

WRITER'S CRAFT

UNIT 5 Courage • **Lesson 3** *A Hole in the Dike*

Cause and Effect

Focus **Cause** and **effect** is when one thing causes another thing to happen.

> ▶ The **cause** is why something happens.
> ▶ The **effect** is what happens.

Identify

Look in "A Hole in the Dike" for the effects listed below. Then write the cause for each.

1. Effect: Peter got off his bike to see what was wrong.

Cause: _____

_____

_____

2. Effect: All the people thanked Peter. They carried him on their shoulders, shouting, "Make way for the hero of Holland! The brave boy who saved our land!"

Cause: _____

_____

_____

UNIT 5 Courage • **Lesson 3** *A Hole in the Dike*

▶ **Cause and Effect**

Practice

Read each sentence. Write the effect (what happened) and the cause (why it happened).

3. Because it was hot, my friends went swimming.

Effect: _____

Cause: _____

4. Since we wanted to be helpful, we picked up our toys.

Effect: _____

Cause: _____

Apply

Write a sentence of your own that shows a cause and an effect. Draw a line under the cause in your sentence.

_____

_____

COMPREHENSION

Commas in Dialogue

There are many places to use commas. One place is in dialogue.

Rule	**Example**
▶ A comma is used before the quotation marks that begin a speaker's exact words.	▶ I said to my dog, "Jump over this log."
▶ A comma is used after the word before the end quotes.	▶ "I want to watch him jump," said my friend Mai.

Read the sentences. Put commas where they belong.

1. Joe said "I need to buy some carrots."

2. Charlotte sighed "Tomorrow is another day."

3. "I cannot sell my cat" I said.

4. I added "I will give her to you as a present."

5. I said "I want to visit her each Saturday."

▶ **Commas in Dialogue**

MECHANICS

Practice

Write a comma where it is needed in each sentence.

6. Misha said "I don't think this is a treasure map."

7. Sasha replied "Oh, yes it is."

8. Trisha sighed "Some diamonds would be nice."

9. Misha said "Maybe we'll find gold!"

10. "Just some money would suit me fine" said Sasha.

Proofread

Read the story. Write commas where they are missing in the sentences with dialogue. Use proofreading marks.

Once upon a time there were three sisters. Each sister had a cat. One day, a sister said "I would like to have another cat." So the family went to the cat shelter downtown and found a stray cat to take home. The youngest sister said "I am glad we are able to give another cat a home."

UNIT 5 Courage • **Lesson 3** *A Hole in the Dike*

Characterization

> **Characterization** is the writer's way of showing what the characters in a story are like. Writers do this by telling what the characters do, say, think, and feel.

Read each sentence. Decide what the author is trying to show the reader. Write *acts*, *says*, *thinks*, **or** *feels* **on the line.**

1. Dan sighed with regret. _____

2. She thought it was her fault. _____

3. "I can't wait to go home!" said Shelly.

_____

4. She was sick with worry. _____

UNIT 5 Courage • **Lesson 3** *A Hole in the Dike*

▶**Characterization**

Practice

Read the paragraph. Then write the answers to each question.

Tony had to give a report at school. "I don't like speaking in front of the class," Tony said to his mother. Later, Mrs. O'Brien announced, "The next report is by Tony Perez." Tony walked to the front of the class. He began his report. He thought his voice was too loud. He felt his knees shake.

1. How did Tony feel about speaking in front of his class before his report?

_____

2. What did Tony say about speaking in front of his class?

_____

3. How did he act when he began his report?

_____

WRITER'S CRAFT

Name _____ Date _____

▶ Setting

> The **setting** of a story is the time and place in which the story happens.
>
> Settings:
> ▶ A high school in the morning
> ▶ Maine in the fall
> ▶ A book store in 1962

For each topic, tell when and where the story might take place.

1. Topic: A bike ride _____

2. Topic: A concert _____

3. Topic: A party _____

► Setting

Practice

Read the story and answer the questions. Then tell about the setting in your own words.

Our scout troop went for a hike in a forest last summer. The trees were so thick that it was dark, even in the morning! Not one ray of sunlight could get through the trees. Sometimes we couldn't see the trail. We had to follow the forest ranger. The ranger taught us lots of things about the forest. I think I may become a forest ranger.

4. When did this story take place?

_____

5. Where did this story take place?

_____

6. Tell about the setting in your own words.

_____

WRITER'S CRAFT

UNIT 5 Courage • **Lesson 4** *Martin Luther King, Jr.*

Capitalization: Titles and Initials

There are many places to use capital letters. Use capital letters in titles and initials.

Rule	**Example**
▶ Titles in people's names begin with capital letters.	▶ **Mr.** Tilly told us to form a straight line. **Dr.** Jilly gave me a checkup today.
▶ Initials from people's names are capitalized.	▶ **E. B.** White is the author of *Stuart Little*.

Underline three times (≡) each title or set of initials that should be capitalized in the sentences below.

1. John Adams and John q. Adams were both presidents of the United States.

2. The president of the United States is called *mr. President.*

3. Presidents t. Roosevelt and Franklin d. Roosevelt were cousins.

UNIT 5 Courage • **Lesson 4** *Martin Luther King, Jr.*

Capitalization: Titles and Initials

Practice

Write an initial or title in the blank.

4. Our family doctor is _____ Laurel.

5. The soccer coach at our school is _____ Wang-Lui.

6. The gorilla at the zoo was named _____ Big.

7. The veterinarian who takes care of our cats is named _____ Tawney.

8. Did you ever see Jeff's dad, _____ Cole?

Proofread

Read the story below. Underline three times (≡) all the titles of people and all the initials that should be capitalized. Use proofreading marks.

The architect i. m. Pei was born in China in 1917. mr. Pei has designed many large, beautiful buildings. In 1960, he designed the terminal at jfk International Airport in New York. A landscape architect designs gardens and outdoor spaces. The first person to call himself a landscape architect was f. l. Olmsted.

MECHANICS

UNIT 5 Courage • **Lesson 4** *Martin Luther King, Jr.*

Dialogue

> Dialogue tells the reader exactly what the characters say.
>
> **Rules**
>
> Rules for showing what characters are saying:
> - ▶ Put quotation marks (" ") before and after a speaker's exact words.
> - ▶ Always begin the first word of a quotation with a capital letter.
> - ▶ Use a comma to separate a quote from the rest of the sentence.
>
> **Example**
> - ▶ Ken said, "Let's go to the mall."
>
> "That's a great idea," said Pam.

Write two sentences with dialogue and quotation marks.

1. _____

2. _____

▶ **Dialogue**

Practice

Put quotation marks at the beginning and end of the character's words.

1. I like the story about the horse, said Amber.

2. Aren't you glad we know how to read and write? asked Juan.

3. I think she is a really good teacher, Lin declared.

4. Yes! Without her, we wouldn't know how to read, said Scott.

5. I agree, said Deana. She is good!

WRITER'S CRAFT

Sequence

Focus A good writer leads readers through a story.

> ▶ Following the sequence of events helps readers better understand a story.
>
> ▶ Looking for words that show time can help readers follow the sequence of events. Some examples of these words are: *first, then, later*.

Identify

Think about or reread "The Empty Pot." Write down four things that happened in the story. Write them in the order they happened.

1. _____

   _____

2. _____

   _____

   _____

3. _____

   _____

4. _____

   _____

▶ **Sequence**

Practice

Read this paragraph carefully. Then number the pictures in the correct sequence.

Seth gets up every morning at seven o'clock. Every morning he does the same things. He gets dressed first. Then he makes his bed. After that he brushes his teeth. About fifteen minutes later, Seth is ready for breakfast.

_____   _____   _____   _____

Apply

Write sentences about something you know how to do, such as making a sandwich, brushing your teeth, or walking to school. Make sure the sequence of events is clear.

_____

_____

_____

COMPREHENSION

Apostrophes and Colons

Apostrophes and **colons** are special punctuation marks.

Rule	Example
▶ An **apostrophe** is used to make a contraction.	▶ **It's** cold outside. [It is]
▶ An apostrophe is used to form the possessive.	▶ **Jay's** hat was black and gold.
▶ A **colon** is used to introduce a list of items.	▶ Please place these things in your suitcase**:** shoes, socks, shorts, and shirts.
▶ A colon is used in time expressions between the hour and the minutes.	▶ The bus is leaving at **2:45** sharp.

Write the time expression boldfaced in each sentence in numerals on the blank lines after the sentences.

1. At **two-ten**, the doors are locked. _____

2. We must leave the house by **one-thirty**. _____

▶ **Apostrophes and Colons**

MECHANICS

Practice

Read the sentences. Find the words that need apostrophes and colons. Put the apostrophes and colons where they belong.

3. I couldnt agree with you more.

4. These are the best things in life love, music, and friends.

5. A cats life involves a lot of sleep.

6. My dogs favorite toy is my green tennis ball.

Proofread

Write apostrophes and colons where they have been left out in the paragraph below. Use proofreading marks.

Britts backpack was full. He had stuffed it with these things three books, two notebooks, four pens, one pair of gloves, six tennis balls, and two sandwiches. He couldnt find his sandwiches. He was afraid that they might be crushed in the bottom of the backpack. Lunch break was at 1145. He had to hurry to find his lunch.

Sentence Combining

Two sentences with ideas that are alike can be put together or combined by using the word *and*.

Rules

▶ Put a comma before the word *and* when combining sentences.

▶ Do not use *and* to combine two sentences that are not about things that are alike.

Example

▶ Rosa walked to the mailbox, <u>and</u> she mailed the letter.

 **Try It!**

Put an *X* next to the sentences that can be combined because they are on the same topic.

1. The dog barked. He wagged his tail. ____

2. Jason ran home. The sun was shining. ____

3. Seth hit the ball. He ran to first base. ____

4. The car was going fast. We were eating lunch. ____

5. Nick went to the phone. He answered it. ____

Comprehension and Language Arts Skills

Sentence Combining

WRITER'S CRAFT

Practice

Combine these sentences by adding a comma and the word *and*.

1. The monkey jumped. It played.

_____

2. My dad and I went to the store. We bought tennis shoes.

_____

3. Cathy peeled an orange. She ate it.

_____

4. Marta climbed the steps. She slid down the slide.

_____

5. The rabbit picked the carrot. He ate it.

_____

Author's Purpose

Focus Authors write for different reasons. Sometimes they want to give readers information. Sometimes they write to entertain.

Writers *entertain* readers by including
▶ funny words and events
▶ exciting or familiar events
Writers *inform* readers by including
▶ facts that can be proven true
Writers *persuade* readers by including
▶ their opinions
▶ facts to support their opinions
Writers *explain* to readers how to do something by including
▶ the steps in a process

Identify

Reread page 237 of "Brave As a Mountain Lion." What is the author's purpose?

Author's Purpose: _____

How did the author show the purpose? _____

_____

_____

UNIT 5 Courage • **Lesson 6** *Brave As a Mountain Lion*

▶ **Author's Purpose**

COMPREHENSION

Practice

Numbered below are some titles of stories. A list of purposes that authors can use is in the box. Choose the one that best fits each title.

entertain	inform	persuade	explain

1. "Why the School Year Should Be Longer"

_____

2. "The Great Mahooleywhazit and the Big YUCK!"

_____

3. "How to Feed a Baby"

_____

4. "Ocean Animals"

_____

Apply

Choose one of the titles above and write a first sentence for the story.

_____

_____

UNIT 5 Courage • **Lesson 6** *Brave as a Mountain Lion*

Review

▶ Capitalization: I and Proper Nouns

Underline three times the words that should be capital letters.

1. This year i am taking ballet lessons.

2. One day i hope to dance like m. Tallchief.

3. She was part Native american and part scotch-irish.

▶ Conjunctions and Interjections

Underline the conjunctions and circle the interjections in the sentences below.

4. Maine and Vermont are states.

5. Gee! Is New York bordered by New Jersey or Massachusetts?

▶ Commas

Write commas where they are needed.

6. I asked the man "Why isn't your brother going on the train trip?"

7. He said "I hate hearing that clackety-clack!"

8. "I don't like airplanes" said Tommy.

► **Capitalization**

Underline three times the letters that should be capitalized.

I am reading the book *Tiger's Stripes* by j. c. Cole. It is about a young tiger named Tiger jr. He is afraid he is going to lose his stripes if he goes swimming. Since he is afraid, he asks his owl friend, miss Howl. I wonder what he will do!

► **Apostrophes and Colons**

Insert colons and apostrophes where they belong in the sentences below.

9. Three islands are countries Iceland, Greenland, and Australia.

10. Havent you ever heard of Oceania?

11. The conductor said, "The train will depart at 615."

Name _____ Date _____

Time and Order Words

> ▶ You can show time in your writing by telling when things happen.
>
> ▶ Words such as *yesterday*, *tonight*, and *next week* show time.
>
> ▶ You can show order by telling in what order things happen.
>
> ▶ Words such as *first*, *next*, and *finally* show order.

 **Write the time and order words in each sentence.**

1. Yesterday, we decided to buy some fish. _____

2. First, we bought a fish tank. _____

3. Then, we bought fish food. _____

4. Now, we are ready to pick our new pets. _____

5. Tonight, we will go to the pet store to buy

   the fish. _____

UNIT 5 Courage • **Lesson 6** *Brave as a Mountain Lion*

▶ **Time and Order Words**

Practice

Write a sentence using the time or order word next to each number.

6. Finally _____

7. Next week _____

8. First _____

9. Then _____

10. Tomorrow _____

WRITER'S CRAFT

UNIT 6 Our Country and Its People • **Lesson 1** *The First Americans*

▶ Review

▶ Common and Proper Nouns

Read the paragraph below. Circle the common nouns and underline the proper nouns.

There are many types of trees. The Sequoias are one type. They are named after a Cherokee leader. In Arizona, the Petrified Forest is home to many old Sequoia trees. The Coast Redwood, Giant Sequoia, and Dawn Redwood are all types of Sequoias.

▶ Subject and Object Pronouns

Underline the subject pronouns and circle the object pronouns in these sentences.

1. They traveled the world with only one suitcase.

2. We wanted to be like them.

3. She took too many shoes with her.

4. Why can't he take her on his trip?

5. I don't want to go with you.

▶Review

▶**Action Verbs**

Circle the action verbs in the sentences below.

6. Pioneers clear the land.

7. They plant seeds for corn.

8. They dig vegetable gardens.

9. The men and women work hard in the hot sun.

10. The children help their parents.

▶**Possessive Nouns and Pronouns**

Read the sentences below. Fill in the correct possessive form in the blank.

11. _____ name comes from a Native American tribal chief named Seattle. (**Seattle**)

12. _____ tribal group was the Duwamish. (**He**)

13. The _____ location is in Washington. (**city**)

14. _____ brother likes to fish. (**She**)

GRAMMAR AND USAGE

UNIT 6 · **Our Country and Its People** · **Lesson I** *The First Americans*

Audience and Purpose

Your **audience** is the person or people reading your writing.

Your **purpose** is your reason for writing. There are four main purposes for writing.

Rule

▶ To **inform** is to tell facts about something.

▶ To **explain** is to tell how to do something or why something happens.

▶ To **entertain** is to amuse people.

▶ To **persuade** is to talk people into thinking or or doing something.

Example

▶ China is the largest country.

▶ Follow these steps to make a pizza.

▶ The silly puppy fell asleep in the drawer.

▶ Here is why we should not litter.

Try It!   **After each sentence, write the purpose.**

1. If we all help, we can make our city clean. _____

2. As the sun rose, the ocean sparkled like diamonds. _____

3. Here are some simple steps to a better life. _____

4. This is the oldest fossil known to humans. _____

UNIT 6 Our Country and Its People • **Lesson I** *The First Americans*

▶ Audience and Purpose

Practice

For each type of writing, give a possible audience.

5. Fairy tale _____

6. Directions to get to a friend's house

_____

7. Report on United States history

_____

8. Poster for a school bake sale

_____

9. Article about a hockey game

_____

WRITER'S CRAFT

Cause and Effect

Focus When you read, the more you know about what caused something to happen, the better you will understand what you read.

Identify

Read the page from "New Hope." Then tell the cause of the event.

1. Page 269

Event: Lars sailed with his family to this country from Denmark.

Cause: _____

_____

2. Page 276

Event: Lars opened a general store.

Cause: _____

_____

UNIT 6 Our Country and Its People • **Lesson 2** *New Hope*

Cause and Effect

Practice and Apply

For each of the events from "New Hope" listed below, write why it happened.

3. Page 270

Lars bought a wagon, two horses, a hunting rifle, tools, a tent, several bags of seeds, and plenty of food in Minnesota.

Why it happened: _____

_____

4. Page 271

Peter and Mathilde adopted a dog.

Why it happened: _____

_____

_____

5. Page 275

Franz opened a forge.

Why it happened: _____

_____

COMPREHENSION

UNIT 6 Our Country and Its People • **Lesson 2** *New Hope*

Review

Capitalization: Beginnings of Sentences; Months of the Year; Days of the Week

Commas: Words in a Series

Underline three times the letters that should be capitalized. Insert commas where they are needed.

1. The library will be closed on sundays mondays and tuesdays this summer.

2. owls live in trees barns or zoos.

3. Memorial Day is in the month of may.

4. Presidents' Day falls in february.

5. when is Father's Day?

6. winter begins in december in our country.

7. I take long walks on tuesdays thursdays and saturdays.

8. the Midwest has long cold winters.

9. We have fish corn and potatoes on fridays.

10. School will be out in june.

▶ Review

▶ Capitalization and Commas in Greetings

▶ Commas in Closings; City, State, Date

Read the letter. Insert commas where they are needed, and underline three times letters that should be capitalized.

626 Mason Drive
Albany New York
july 1 2001

dear Gerry
    On Monday, I would like to borrow your flag. I need your flag for the parade in our town. I promise to take care of it!

Your cousin
Amy

▶ Quotation Marks and Underlining

Read the sentences below. Add quotation marks and underlining where needed.

11. Recycling helps the environment, said our teacher.

12. She read to us from a book titled Nature and the Environment.

13. I said, We need to recycle our trash.

MECHANICS

Words of Request

> To get someone to do something, it helps to ask in a polite way. Words of request help you do this.
>
> Words of Request:
> ▶ Please
> ▶ Could you
> ▶ Would you
> ▶ May I

 **Circle the words of request in each sentence.**

1. Would you mind sending me a sample?

2. Please come to my party.

3. May I go to the movies?

4. Could you help me move the desk?

5. May I please have more information?

Words of Request

Practice

Write questions using words of request for each situation.

6. Ask for help with your homework.

_____

7. Ask your parents if they will let you stay the night at a friend's house.

_____

8. Ask a salesperson to refund your money.

_____

9. Ask someone to help you find your lost bike.

_____

10. Ask for help lifting something heavy.

_____

WRITER'S CRAFT

UNIT 6 Our Country and Its People • **Lesson 3** *A Place Called Freedom*

Review

Kinds of Sentences

Read each sentence below. Insert the correct end mark. Then write *D* if the sentence is a statement. Write *Q* if the sentence asks a question. Write *I* if the sentence gives a direction or a command. Write *E* if the sentence is an exclamatory sentence.

1. Don't rock the boat _____

2. Where is your life jacket _____

3. The water is blue and calm today _____

4. Look how far we can see across the lake _____

Linking and Helping Verbs

Underline the linking verbs and circle the helping verbs in each sentence.

5. Texas is not the largest state.

6. In 1959 it was the largest state.

7. Then Alaska was made a state.

8. Now Alaska is the largest state.

▶Review

GRAMMAR AND USAGE

▶ Subject/Verb Agreement

Correct the underlined verbs so they agree with the subjects.

The Sahara Desert <u>are</u> the largest in the world. It <u>are</u> in Africa. The word *Sahara* is Arabic for *desert*. Not many plants <u>grows</u> in the Sahara.

▶ Parts of Sentences

Underline the subject once and the predicate twice.

9. My great-grandmother came to this country on a ship.

10. They brought food with them for the trip.

▶ Complete Sentences

Change the run-on phrases into a complete sentence.

11. Tokyo capital of Japan.

_____

UNIT 6 Our Country and Its People • **Lesson 3** *A Place Called Freedom*

Structure of Scripts

▶ A **script** is a group of sentences that tells people what to say.

▶ The words in a script should be short and to the point.

▶ Scripts also tell people what to do. These are the **stage directions.** The stage directions are usually put in ( ) or [ ].

▶ Scripts are used in movies, TV shows, and plays.

Todd: (enters the room) How are you today, Mrs. Kurtz?

Mrs. Kurtz: I'm great! It's good to see you, Todd.

 **Read the script lines. Circle the letter of the line that is short and to the point.**

1. **A.** It seemed like we had to walk forever and ever.
   B. We walked for a long time.

2. **A.** The train is late!
   B. I can't believe the train is not running on time!

3. **A.** I wanted to ask you if you have seen Carlos today.
   B. Have you seen Carlos today?

UNIT 6 Our Country and Its People • **Lesson 3** *A Place Called Freedom*

► **Structure of Scripts**

Practice

Write a short script for the following example. Add stage directions.

Example: Dan and Zack are talking about last night's homework.

Dan: _____

Zack: _____

Dan: _____

Zack: _____

WRITER'S CRAFT

Review

Adjectives and Adverbs

Circle the adjectives and underline the adverbs in the sentences below.

1. The red lines on the map are highways.

2. Black dots usually represent cities.

3. Capitals are clearly shown with white stars.

4. There are fifty states on the map.

5. The map uses five colors for the states.

Circle the articles in the following sentences.

6. Green trees are the symbol for parks.

7. The brown triangles mean tall mountains.

8. There was a red square for a school.

9. Fold the map carefully.

10. I used an orange marker to highlight our trip.

►**Review**

GRAMMAR AND USAGE

►**Singular and Plural Nouns**

Circle the singular nouns and underline the plural nouns in each sentence.

11. How many giraffes are in the zoo?

12. They say that a cat has nine lives.

13. The house has five windows.

14. There are two full moons this month.

15. Put the toys for charity in these two boxes.

►**Adverbs**

Read the following paragraph. Underline the adverbs.

The violin is part of the string family of instruments. Yesterday, I learned that the viola, cello, and double bass are also part of the violin family. Harmonics can be played by lightly placing your hand on the strings. Orchestras always have violins in them.

Words of Request

To get someone to do something, it helps to ask in a polite way. Words of request help you do this.

Words of Request:
▶ Please
▶ Could you
▶ Would you
▶ May I

 **Underline the words of request in each sentence.**

1. May I please have a piece of the apple?

2. Could you help me carry my books?

3. May I stay up until 10:00 tonight?

4. Please bring muffins to the bake sale.

5. Would you ask if I could go too?

▶ **Words of Request**

WRITER'S CRAFT

Practice

Write five questions using words of request.

6.

7.

8.

9.

10.

Review

▶ Capitalization: *I*, Proper Nouns, People's Titles and Initials

Underline three times the letters that should be capitalized.

1. Today i read a book about the american Revolution.

2. The british army was one of the best in the world.

3. Congress asked general George washington to lead the troops.

▶ Conjunctions and Interjections

Circle the conjunctions and underline the interjections in the sentences below.

4. The Snake River flows westward, and the Missouri River flows eastward.

5. Oh! I forgot to study geography last night.

6. Do it this morning or at lunchtime.

▶Review

▶ Commas in Dialogue

Add commas where they belong in each sentence.

7. I told the captain "Aye, aye, sir."

8. G. M. Cohan said "I'm a Yankee Doodle Dandy."

9. "I saw a great movie last night" explained Timothy.

▶ Apostrophes

Insert apostrophes where they belong in each sentence.

10. Switzerlands mountains are beautiful.

11. We couldnt climb to the very top.

12. The countrys people speak three languages.

▶ Colons

Write colons where they belong in each sentence.

13. My favorite television program starts at 500.

14. These animals were in the show dogs, pigs, cats, and birds.

15. I will be leaving at 445 today.

MECHANICS

UNIT 6 Our Country and Its People • **Lesson 6** *A Piece of Home*

Supporting Details

> ▶ The **main idea** is the topic of the paragraph.
> ▶ **Supporting details** tell about the main idea.
>
> Main Idea: Hawaii is a beautiful place.
> Details:
> ▶ The beaches are breathtaking.
> ▶ There are grand mountains.
> ▶ Hawaii has colorful trees and flowers.

Try It!

Read the main idea below. Then cross out the one sentence that does not tell about the main idea.

Main Idea: Toby is a smart dog.

Details: • He fetches the newspaper every morning.
• Toby is a black lab.
• He can catch a biscuit in the air.
• He can push the button on an elevator for the correct floor.

UNIT 6 Our Country and Its People • **Lesson 6** *A Piece of Home*

▶ Supporting Details

Practice

Write three details about the main idea below.

Main Idea: There is a lot to do in the winter.

_____

_____

_____

_____

_____

_____

_____

WRITER'S CRAFT

Name _____ Date _____

Fact and Opinion

Focus Writers talk to readers through their stories. To make their stories interesting, writers use facts and opinions.

> ▶A **fact** is something that can be proven true. It is a fact that jalapeños grow on plants.
>
> ▶An **opinion** is what someone thinks or feels. It is an opinion if someone says jalapeños taste good.

Identify

Look back at "Jalapeño Bagels." Copy one sentence that gives a fact. Copy one sentence that gives an opinion.

Fact

1. _____

_____

Opinion

2. _____

_____

Practice

Read this paragraph. Draw a line under each sentence that tells a fact. Circle the sentences that give opinions.

    Jamie was born in the United States. His parents were born in Mexico. They moved to the United States ten years ago. His parents are wonderful. They have taught him how to speak two languages. It is important to know more than one language. That way he can talk to more people.

Apply

Write several sentences about your favorite food. Make sure you include some facts and some opinions.

_____

_____

_____

_____

_____

_____

COMPREHENSION

Review

Sentences: End Marks

Subjects and Predicates

Circle the subject and underline the predicate in the sentences below. Then, add the correct end mark.

1. Many Irish people in the 1800s relied on potatoes for food

2. Their crops failed so many times

Common and Proper Nouns

Circle the common nouns and underline the proper nouns in these sentences.

3. Panda bears live in China.

4. China has loaned the United States two bears.

Plural Nouns

Circle the correct plural noun from the two boldfaced words in each sentence.

5. All the **children childs** helped in the garden.

6. The **boys boyes** raked the dirt.

▶ **Review**

▶ **Linking and Action Verbs**

▶ **Present and Past Tense**

**Look at the word in boldface. Circle *Past*
or *Present* at the end of each sentence.**

7. People **were playing** board games 4,000
   years ago.   **Past   Present**

8. Chess **is played** with figures of the king,
   queen, and bishop.   **Present   Past**

▶ **Adjectives and Adverbs**

**Circle the adjectives and underline the
adverbs in each sentence.**

9. Yellow parakeets make nice pets.

10. Many birds sing beautifully.

▶ **Contractions and Conjunctions**

**Circle the contractions and underline the
conjunctions in the sentences.**

11. Games and sports take practice to learn.

12. Many sports aren't easy to master.

MECHANICS

Plagiarism

> **Plagiarism** is using someone else's ideas or statements as your own. It is important that you write papers using your own words.

 **Rewrite each sentence in your own words.**

1. The largest animal that lives on land is the African elephant.

   _____

   _____

2. The fastest land animal, the cheetah, runs at 70 miles per hour.

   _____

   _____

3. In the desert lives the bobcat.

   _____

   _____

▶ **Plagiarism**

Practice

Read the paragraph. Then rewrite it in your own words.

Pluto is the smallest planet. It is much smaller than the other planets. It is 1,413 miles wide. That may not seem very small, but compare it to the biggest planet, Jupiter. It is 88,732 miles wide. Pluto is also the coldest planet. It is so cold that nothing could live there.

_____

_____

_____

_____

WRITER'S CRAFT